# GIRAFFES
# AT THE ZOO

By Finn Ward

Gareth Stevens
PUBLISHING

**Please visit our website, www.garethstevens.com. For a free color catalog of all our high-quality books, call toll free 1-800-542-2595 or fax 1-877-542-2596.**

**Library of Congress Cataloging-in-Publication Data**

Ward, Finn.
  Giraffes at the zoo / Finn Ward.
    pages cm. — (Zoo animals)
  Includes index.
  ISBN 978-1-4824-2593-2 (pbk.)
  ISBN 978-1-4824-2594-9 (6 pack)
  ISBN 978-1-4824-2595-6 (library binding)
  1. Giraffe—Juvenile literature. 2. Zoo animals—Juvenile literature.  I. Title.
  SF408.6.G57W37 2016
  599.638—dc23

                              2015002595

First Edition

Published in 2016 by
**Gareth Stevens Publishing**
111 East 14th Street, Suite 349
New York, NY 10003

Editor: Ryan Nagelhout
Designer: Katelyn E. Reynolds

Photo credits: Cover, p. 1 Phongkrit/Shutterstock.com; p. 5 Nadia Borisevich/Shutterstock.com; p. 7 Diola/ Shutterstock.com; p. 9 sevenke/Shutterstock.com; pp. 11, 13, 24 (neck) Evgeniya Uvarova/Shutterstock.com; pp. 15, 24 (spot) Peter O'Toole/Shutterstock.com; p. 17 Julia Xanthos/NY Daily News Archive/Getty Images; pp. 19, 24 (leaves) ilovezion/Shutterstock.com; p. 21 Thitisan/Shutterstock.com; p. 23 Joy Brown/Shutterstock.com.

Printed in the United States of America

CPSIA compliance information: Batch #CS15GS: For further information contact Gareth Stevens, New York, New York at 1-800-542-2595.

# Contents

The zoo is full
of animals.

Giraffes live
at the zoo!

They walk on four legs.

They have long necks.

11

They like to live
in groups.

Giraffes have lots of hair.
It has brown spots on it.

15

Zoos take care of them.

Giraffes love
to eat leaves.

Some zoos let you feed them!

Baby giraffes are cute.
They are called calves.

23

# Words to Know

leaves

neck

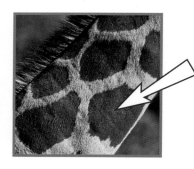
spot

# Index

24